The Making of Me

Rebecca Tupn

SWEETSPIRE LITERATURE
MANAGEMENT

Contents

Thank you to everybody for keeping me sane, grounded and who have listened to me! To my mum who never fails to be there, my brother Simon and my wonderful sister in law Te Aroha and little niece Kahuirere and my nephew Elijah! Thank you very much for chatting to me, reassuring me, helping me out and for always being there! I am so thankful xxxxx

Also want to thank my friend Andy who helped me out with my car and with tidying up my yard and my house – thanks so much!

Also thank you to my partner Brent, definitely unlike anyone I have met before, we have good times and I want to thank you for always being there and having my back, I appreciate you very much!!!!!

Thank you to Sky Fitness Moray Place owner Phil, Iron Warriors Nick, Dave and Rob (also to the polytechnic students/fellow gym warriors at Sky Fitness 24 gym.)

Thank you to the nurses who give me my six-weekly Tysabri infusion you ladies are wonderful, super helpful and very kind.

I also want to thank my family and friends that I do not see that often, this adult life gets busy and chaotic at times so I hope to see you all again sometime xxx

To Jamie the work broker at Ministry of Social Development – thank you for being so helpful when I was looking for work! It took me over a year to find work but you were so supportive. Thanks again!!!

I also have enjoyed working with all of the charities over the years because I love working with all sorts of people and interacting with everybody and anybody. I put myself out there because I have always enjoyed working with others. I feel lucky I have always had a roof over my head; I was fed and was never alone at Christmas. I am aware people are not as lucky as me and I am grateful, full of empathy and I want to give back to society.

If these last two years have taught me anything – it was to BE KIND ALWAYS!!!! I also want to share my story because I had a few years that I wish on nobody…it was emotional, horrible and I mostly want everyone to know – that bad times do not last forever!

Thank you for reading and please do reach out for help if times are particularly bad! Life is for living and if we reach out to family, friends, our doctor or counselling – these can help us all. We are not alone (even if it feels like we are). Someone does care!

CHAPTER ONE

Welcome, this is me!

HELLO MY NAME is Rebecca Tupu and I am thirty eight years old. My mum is a New Zealand European and my dad is a Samoan man that came to New Zealand in the 1970's. I also have a younger brother. We also lost my younger sister when I was six to cot death.

I have lived in Dunedin my whole life and thanks to my Mum, my brother and I went to Catholic schools for primary and high school. I went to school, was good at reading and writing but bad at maths then was late learning how to swim at eleven.

I did a junk mail delivery when I was eleven in 1997, my mum helped me and my brother did too sometimes. (Or maybe we all loved buying fish and chips over half of our work done, down the road. We ate the chips, chatted, had a rest then finished my mail delivery.) I was also proud to buy my Learners driving licence with my junk mail money. I did the run until I was sixteen when I gave the junk mail run to my brother.

In my family, we all love music. Mum would listen to the radio as my brother and I ate our breakfast before school, Dad loved listening to his tapes or cds as he had a beer after work or in the weekend. Mum, me and my brother loved concerts/outdoor music gatherings and listening to the stereo. In our older lives my brother and I love our Bluetooth speakers and car stereos.

At primary school I loved it when we got raffle books in the 1990s – I would walk around the neighbourhood and sell a book of ten rafles, collect the money, chat and then I would take the money home then return it to my school. I would often ask for another book so I could sell more. I do not think though these days if I had children I would let them sell rafles. Things were a bit easier and safer then I think.

At sixteen I also got my first job at a big grocery warehouse, I was so excited to get "real money". I worked there while I was Year twelve and thirteen at Kavanagh College. A highlight of that time was me buying my ticket to the Red Hot Chili Peppers at QE2 Park that was in Christchurch.

I had bought my eighty five dollar general admission ticket, showed my parents and they were not happy that I wanted to go to Christchurch by myself. In the end my mum came to Christchurch with me, bless her! At the concert also got upgraded to "The Chili Bin" aka mosh pit – great times!!!!

Me and a few friends were talking about our Year Twelve high school formal coming up. My friends did not want to go because we did not have dates. I spoke up and said that we needed to go to the formal; otherwise I think that we would regret it when we were older. We ended up getting our dresses, had fun and hung out with ourselves and others! One of the girls ended up going out with a guy the year above us afterwards.

Also in my Year Twelve year we had to vote for someone who showed kindness for the Christian Citizenship Award. I voted for this lovely girl who was in my German class, we both played netball, were friendly when we saw each other; she was so smiley and kind. I thought nothing of it after voting and said if they did not have it written down on prize giving day (in front of the school gymnasium) if I was not getting an academic award at prize giving I was not attending. In the end they gave the Citizenship prize doubly to the girl I voted for and me! I pointed to the board and was like "What the hell? That is me!!!" At prize giving they said that this year was different, they had two people who were voted for my year twelve for this award, so they decided to give it to both of us. To this day I still have the certificate and the beautiful bible they gave me. We had Peer Support training for Year Thirteen the next day; we did activities and affirmations for each other on "concertina style" paper. I opened mine and people wrote congratulating me on my award and they said they voted for me. It was really nice to read later.

After high school in 2004 I went to Dunedin College of Education because I wanted to be a primary school teacher. Then I changed my mind and did a Social Work Degree at Otago University and I did a Level Four Mental Health Support Work Certificate at Otago Polytechnic, proudly graduating from them in August and December 2010. I was also the first one of my friends to have their restricted licence and car then at twenty I got my full licence. I loved the freedom of being able to drive and to this day I can only drive an automatic car.

When I was at the grocery warehouse, I grew comfortable with life, too comfortable. I did love my friend's there, loved the social club they used to run (One dollar a week single membership or two dollars double membership, I had the latter to take a friend or bring a guy friend to have people guessing if that guy who came with me was my boyfriend or not? Haha!!!)

I lived in a neighbourhood with nosy neighbours and interesting people who would visit my partner and me at my house. I had some well- meaning older ladies speaking to me and saying "You have qualifications, why are you not using them?". I had a think, yes why was I not using them? I did apply for jobs and finally a mental health firm employed me in October 2013. I loved working with the residents/ clients in that job and seeing them happy and progressing well in their lives.

I loved volunteering in Lifeline's "Wellness Tent" at Rhythm and Vines festival in Gisborne at New Year's 2018 into 2019. We gave out fruit infused water, condoms and sold people kambucha and bliss balls and we scanned their bracelet that was loaded with money. It was a good time and I enjoyed talking to people and finding people from all over New Zealand and beyond! So much fun and I did get to escape to the 2019 countdown at midnight! One of my very treasured memories.

So yes, life was full of work, paying bills, always out there, always doing something, being happy, my partner/ex-husband (talk about him later!) my family, friends, travelling, having the odd bourbon, going to concerts, volunteer work with numerous charities around my job, doing quarter marathons/half marathon walks and I love those positive sayings/ mantras on posters, books and cups. I was not into creating problems for people and I did not go and create any unnecessary drama, I chose to steer away from that.

No, I did not know at the end of 2019 I was going to be called to Endocrinology and be told that I "may have multiple sclerosis". Now I think of it I did have traces of the "foot drop" you get with MS but I explained it to my doctor and she said it could be from when I had a twenty kilogram of weight loss a few years back (done by going to gym classes often and cutting carbs) and it could be my body reacting to that?

I took my mum and ex-husband to that appointment. We were there and we wanted to know why we were not having any babies. I had a MRI scan earlier and I had been told I was not ovulating, and upon being told about possibly having multiple sclerosis I was thinking "Am I going to die? What if I die? I am so scared" I was anxious, crying a few times worrying and I got a letter in the mail later saying it may take six weeks to get an appointment with a neurologist at Dunedin Hospital. I did not know anything about multiple sclerosis, I could remember volunteering and doing a street annual appeal for Multiple Sclerosis Otago one time but that was all. I was a ball of nerves wondering what was wrong with me.

Little did I know what lay ahead for me, my extreme life changes, life firsts and extreme emotions that I never would wish on anyone!!!! Sure these things happen every day to people, though it was like a massive snowball effect for me, one after another and it seemed like my whole life was falling apart in front of me. I am sharing my story with people today because I acknowledge things were horrible but with the right supports we can come out of it, we live, we learn and become stronger.

CHAPTER TWO

MS diagnosis

I FINALLY GOT the neurologist appointment and I took my mum and ex- husband again. I remember the neurologist showing me pictures of my brain, we saw scarring or lesions on my brain, he mentioned my cerebellum and I was introduced to the MS nurse and was told I can contact them anytime if I had concerns or there was any change to my symptoms.

Also at the end of this month we went and looked at my (now) house that is rural out of Dunedin. It seemed a long way out of town and I had never been there before. The house was big and it had three bedrooms. The lady who owned the house before was an artist and I saw one of the biggest artist easels I had seen in my life. There were so many trees around the house and it looked pretty. The nature looked nice and it looked like a great place on a summer's day.

The reason we looked at the open home was simple – the rental market in Dunedin was super expensive, they ran so many invasive checks on you and it was horrible searching for a place. We had gone to a few banks and just because we were only on my income it was out of the question to buy a house in Dunedin. We had gone to two big banks, declined and I got very upset at the ex-husband who was suggesting we should quit looking for a house. I said we will go to a mortgage advisor, if we are declined there I will be quiet about wanting to own a house. I hated the renting process with a passion! Having landlords come onto your property with no notice (one quite often did), slightly failing the odd inspection and them not so promptly fixing things sometimes. It was my dream to own my own house one day so I would never have to rent again. We did get approved for the mortgage; funny thing was…it was from another major bank.

My mum and I were going on a Pacific Island cruise to Samoa, American Samoa, Fiji and Tonga in April 2020. I was so excited in my thirty four years I was finally going to get to my half ethnicity to see Samoa. Covid started becoming a big problem and that trip was cancelled. (Took over a year to get reimbursed for that trip and mum and I both had Dunedin to Auckland return tickets and Air New Zealand held those fares in credit.)

Late March 2020, it was announced New Zealand was having a lockdown due to the Coronavirus. We had to stay home unless we were an essential worker, shopping, accessing healthcare or outside going for a walk near our home. I was an essential worker who worked in a twenty four hour supported accommodation. It was weird with nobody on the streets and it was quick to get to work. I did love how somebody came up with the idea to put teddies in your window so children and their families could appreciate seeing multiple teddy bears in the neighbourhood on their daily exercise. It was so nice, so colourful and you did get the odd positive comment.

In the end of April 2020, I had an MS relapse. My left foot was constantly dragging and dropping and it was getting very annoying.

I called the MS nurse, who told me to call my doctor so I did. I called my doctor and I went to see him and he referred me to my neurologist. I was given five hundred milligrams of the steroid prednisone to take at night for five nights and some omeprazole for my stomach. I was told that I will not get a good sleep on this so I got the week off work with a medical certificate.

I was not able to move into my mortgaged house until beginning of Level Two (New Zealand had four levels of dealing with this virus and Level Two was close to normal, Level One was normal) but this was changed to end of Level Three in May 2020. There was a clause in my house sale document that said the vendor selling the house could stay there during lockdown and until we could move in. This was very stressful, I had MS symptoms due to the stress, and because I was the breadwinner I was very anxious and unhappy that my sickness-filled husband had never gotten a part time or casual job despite my many reminders. He was coming up with weird-and-wonderful ideas of what to fix in the house and I wondered where we were going to get that money from. I finally mustered up the courage to say we should end our marriage and he was not happy but he made arrangements to go back up north to his hometown and be with his family.

Towards the end my ex-husband was rude; he argued with my mum and argued with me. It got so hostile with him, I told my friend and she said she would call the police about him. The police came and spoke to us; I had to have time off work due to the ex-husband causing grief. Do you know how hard it was to prove "domestic violence" was happening? My work took that time off my normal annual leave and I argued about what he did to me and my mum. They said I needed proof of the phone calls and I got a bit of paper saying that we did call but due to the privacy act, it did not say what we had called about. It should not be this hard for someone to back track and get this information in order to be paid for needed time off work – when my mum and I were victims.

CHAPTER THREE

Post Marriage 2020

THERE WERE SEVERAL things that happened – I got 2 big boxes from Pack and Send and packed the forty two inch television to return to the ex- husband. (Had some sentimental value too because the ex-husband's 90 year old army veteran grandfather passed away and gave the ex- husband, his siblings and his cousins two thousand dollars, five hundred dollars each. He spent that money on food, PlayStation games and an eight hundred dollar television from JB Hi-Fi. He also spent a thousand dollars on paying for my cars back brakes to be fixed at that time too because they were low and I could not afford to save any money.) So I felt better having sent his three boxes back to him. I had some people say to me I should have burned or sold his things but I could not bring myself to do that, it is not my nature. I needed to get his things away from me soon for my own wellbeing like remembering our good times and maybe regretting that I had sent him away. He had gotten back on the benefit back home and we together agreed to pay half each to send these things.

It was a relief to finally have the ex -husband out of my life, I could relax and not have to listen to the many dreams that he wanted to do with the house – ultimately to be paid for by myself. I had more money in my pocket; I did not have to support somebody anymore who was used to not working and used the excuse "nobody wants to employ me!"

Also with my old rented house we had to move quickly end of May 2020 and it ended up I still had to pay mortgage money and my old rental's rent. I turned out I could make mortgage payment and rates but half of my fortnight rental payment. You see people were not too excited about my old rental - there still is a housing crisis yes, it was 2 bedrooms but was old, cold, not the prettiest, got mice a few times, dark and there was loads of stairs. In the end they made the bathroom look nice and somebody finally got the house.

There was leftover bond money because they touched it to pay my first time ever rent arrears. I paid for the bond myself and they did end up giving half to me and half to the ex-husband because he was listed on the tenancy. I was angry because he received a free three hundred dollars that he did not pay for.

In my new house I inherited lots of things because old owner wanted to sell up, live her gypsy-art lifestyle and leave New Zealand. She left couches, bookshelves, a bed, old style day beds, crockery, cutlery, gardening equipment and my mum and I had lots of cleaning to do because the lady left lots of mess. I also had a mate who cut my hedges, water blasted my driveway, cut my bench and removed the skirting board because new oven did not fit in the oven space (crazy story) and he helped me so much. In October 2020, I invited a few friends for my thirty fifth birthday celebration and delayed house warming. A few people come by to my day time party; I was so grateful they come along and I was nice to chill, relax, eat birthday food, then we had some cold beverages and chatted.

Yes and later on I did join some of the singles sites – such as Badoo and Tinder. It was fun chatting to guys and seeing what we had in common. Could we be friends or more? I did try going out with a few guys but their main issue was time. All I asked for was a good morning/good night text and to see them two or three times a week. Hmmm…even once a week catch up was difficult from their end sometimes, so in the end I ended these liasions too. Surely there was a decent guy out there? This cannot be all. I thought I am a good person who just wants companionship, somebody to be affectionate with and ultimately grow to love, to be together with for a long time. Is that such a big thing to ask for?

CHAPTER FOUR

My Life Is Falling Apart!

IT WAS JANUARY 2021 and I was contently relaxing in my lounge on my day off work. Then shock horror there was an email from a lawyer representing my ex-husband. She said I should get a hold of my lawyer so I emailed my lawyer and mortgage broker. My ex-husband's lawyer said it was for the Separation Marital Law and saying that now we are separated it was only appropriate to divide our assets. They spoke of my house and my car and I was horrified that it was all my money that paid for this - and I could be losing some or all of it. I broke down crying and I told my mum what I had just received. Yes she agreed with me that it all was mine because I went to work and earned it and he never made a move to get any sort of work.

I do remember that one of my dear friends she came to my house (for her first time) because we both had time off work. I was so shaken and together we fit photos into frames and made collages for my lounge wall. That was so therapeutic and I thanked her so much for coming with me to my house, that was so beautiful and I will never ever forget that.

Also a few times this year I utilised the Employee Assistance Programme through work. You could have up to three appointments and if you needed more you could ask your workplace for it. I liked talking to an experienced counsellor who listened to you, acknowledged your feelings and sometimes you could not help but cry but that was a safe place to do that.

I did feel sometimes that I needed someone to talk to in the small hours so I would call Lifeline or 1737 if I needed someone to talk to or listen to me, just that chat would make me feel better and I am so grateful those services were there for me in that dark time. They did ask me some safety questions and I said I am not suicidal, I just need to talk thank you. I must say for me I have an "eternal optimistic" streak in me that is always there, swear there is somebody watching over me. I also believe that although life can be rough at times, things do get better. Not instantly but slowly things will improve, believe me I know this!

My health was getting worse over the year, with my multiple worries and things kept happening to me constantly. May 2021 came and in the same week I was sent two big crushing lots of news. My work wanted to dismiss me due to my health and the Separation Marital Law was finished. I got to keep my house and my car and I had to pay my ex-husband thirteen thousand dollars. I was relieved that I got to keep my car and my house. I was given some change from my lawyer so to celebrate I went to Queenstown and did the Nevis Bungy at Queen's Birthday weekend. (Oh and we did a cheeky K Mart visit since Dunedin did not have one anymore.) I had already done the Kawarau and the Ledge Bungy's – my certificates proudly sit on my wall.

In July 2021 I received my medical dismissal from my job of almost eight years. It was very hard to take, I was so upset. I either worked or studied, working was now what I did because I did not want to add to my decent sized student loan. I also declined to come to the farewell morning tea that they would hold for worker's that left. I had seen many of these in my time but you see everyone who left was going to a new job somewhere. Not leaving to become unemployed. I felt really horrible that I answered a senior workers email saying that I did not want a farewell morning tea thank you.

In September 2021 I was put on my first ever benefit in twenty years. It took a bit of getting used to. Not having a regular place to go for work, I loved that job and there was also the financial difference of working and not working – this new lifestyle was not for me.

Also there was a lovely but sad moment; I became pregnant for the first time at 36. It was eight years since first trying; I was told for a few years that I was not ovulating so I just put it down to that I could never get pregnant. I did feel some cramps before knowing I was pregnant and my periods were weird due to stress. I did a test and it came back that I was pregnant. Wow, I was looking forward to this to be able to make my mum a grandma, brother and his girlfriend uncle, aunty and godparents. Sadly baby was not to be. It was described that the little sac baby was in had no heartbeat and baby was given the name Ashley – so baby can always be remembered for the six-seven weeks they were inside me for. I was quite upset and mourning what would have been. The week after I had my procedure to clear baby matter, it was lucky that I had already signed up to do a Friday and Saturday two hours of the Breast Cancer Appeal. It was nice to see people, chat and be distracted from my trauma of losing wee Ashley, otherwise I would have been at home dwelling on it and crying. I have always loved to keep busy. Well I am glad in the knowledge of Ashley being here briefly that this is proof that I can get pregnant sometime again.

I really do want to get back to work sometime in the future because I do feel that I have it in me to go to work. I also have had the feeling that I have been lucky with all that I have had in my life so I want to continue helping however I can to put some kindness and goodness into the world.

CHAPTER FIVE

The Show Must Go On

SO, LIFE AFTER all this has been a struggle at times. I do think I am lucky that I already have it ingrained in me that I am very lucky and optimistic, I have always maintained a positive outlook when problems do arise and I work at it to fix whatever is wrong like talk to family, friends or a professional. There are the odd tears and or discussions. I do like to find things to laugh at because laughter is so healthy and it lifts your spirits.

My multiple sclerosis has meant a lot of adjustment and getting used to whatever it throws at me. I did have a relapse in April 2020 where my left foot was dropping, it was tired and I was tripping over my left foot. I was having trouble walking so I contacted my doctor, who referred me to my neurologist. I then received an appointment (during the national lockdown due to the health sue Covid, that many places experienced around the world.) and I was given 500 milligrams of prednisone for five nights and some omeprazole for my stomach. They did warn me that I may have trouble sleeping so I got a medical certificate to take the week off work.

As well as my left drop foot I felt tired quicker and had the urgency to pass urine often. So sometimes when I got very tired my body ached and I got my foot drop would occur. I would call the multiple sclerosis nurses if anything was out of the ordinary, or I told them about my marriage ending or anything like that.

I also joined multiple sclerosis pages online and I got in contact with the local MS society.

I did get it explained to me that multiple sclerosis was like a plastic cord. Say that my nerves were covered with the layer on top of a cord, the layer was called myelin and my own immune cells were attacking the myelin that was protecting my nerves. The "cord" would short out causing pain within my body. Yes and any one Multiple Sclerosis experiencing it differently.

I went on the public health funded Tysabri in November 2020. I would get a normal drip that would put Tysabri in my body, it took around two hours but needed to give three hours when I started. They also test you for the "John Cunningham Virus" -if you test positive your medication given to you changes. I was negative to it but this can change for anybody.

I was always hearing that you need to tell the neurologists and nurses if you plan to have a baby because you will need extra care while you are pregnant. I was often asking the nurses about this because I did still want to have babies at thirty four and thirty five years. I always wondered if I could have a baby and for some people their multiple sclerosis symptoms change, get better or get worse.

I have had around three MRI's that let the neurologist or doctor know how my symptoms are. On my last yearly one, I was told there were no more new issues, so I was happy and shared with my online people experiencing the same things as me. You lie down in a very small cell that they can gather information what is happening with your body, then your medical professional makes an appointment to see you. I have been told from my last MRI that there is no further damage done to my brain because of my Tysabri infusions that I get once a month.

Sometimes you feel a bit sad or have "grief" about things you used to do but are not as able to do them anymore. Yes you do feel sad or miss doing these, I used to enjoy walking but now it is too sore and I get tired quicker. I used to be a person who was rarely at home, was out and about, was visiting friends and had so much energy. Now I have to conserve my energy and identify the times that I feel most tired or not tired.

CHAPTER SIX

My ex-husband

HE USED TO be my best friend, someone to laugh with and we both had the dream of having babies. I used to think he was the one but looking back he never had work, he always loved television, computer games, radio and he was a bit narcissistic. I did love him and was blinded about him having a free ride on my time and money.He did always talk about marriage, I was unsure about changing my surname, he would not stop talking about it, it wore me down, so we went to the registry and I ended up taking his name. He did tell me that he wanted me to change my surname so that "our whole family would have the same last name." I wanted to get my tertiary qualifications, travel and have fun before babies. We were both twenty three when we met and I told him age thirty I will have babies.

We did have a hard time conceiving. He had a low sperm count, I went to Endocrinology at the hospital and I was told I was not ovulating. We also went to seek fertility IVF treatment but there was too many hurdles. I always wanted a baby, I love children and I love working with children, watching them grow. I was never sure when or if we would have babies and it turned out that we did not have any children, People tell me that I am lucky we did not have children and that I "dodged a bullet" there.

I always asked him to look for a part time job since he had sickness issues but nothing ever happened. There was a time when he had an appointment and wanted to use my car. He dropped me off at my afternoon shift work, then I had finished and he was not there. I found out he was asleep so I angrily told him to come and get me because I was tired and hungry. I had to think long and hard before I lent him my car again.

The year 2020 came and with lockdown, getting the house and listening to his grandiose stories of what he wanted to do to the house, I finally ended our marriage. He left Dunedin and went up north. He is the person who ended our conversations and I heard that he got a delivery boy job. Yes and I was so upset he was going to try and take my house and my car, I did not know what was happening and the suspense was palpable.

I can get divorced in May 2022 which will be great so I can move on with my life. I still have his surname on my driver's licence and on my house title. In New Zealand you must be separated for two years and you can apply for divorce together or separately. In my case it is going to be separately, because he has childishly chosen to not speak to me and also because he lives in the North Island and I am in the South Island. I will have to get somebody to present him the papers and to sign a declaration about giving him the papers.

I had always said that I was not going to leave Dunedin because it was my hometown, my family and friends are here, and my job was here. He said he stayed here because I refused to move. He also did not believe in divorce, he said many years ago he would not do it ever.

He also spoke about his own parents have been separated thirty plus years, they live on the opposite side of town to each other and they will never divorce. So I have about six months until I can actually apply and I am going to be applying as soon as I legally can because that part of my life is well and truly over.

CHAPTER SEVEN

Unemployment

BEING UNEMPLOYED REALLY did hit me hard. I loved my old job and I worked so well with the resident's there. It was an eleven or twelve person mental health service and a lot of people never or rarely did see their families. There were a few people whose family came to visit and it was nice to see. We were like their family, they would miss us in our work weekend or if we had time off work due to our work holidays.

I loved spending Christmas Day with the work residents too – they loved receiving the present that we bought them and they loved the food we served them. I loved working with the residents, setting goals and working on the goals. I loved to see the residents happy as well.

I was dismissed from my job on the 1st July 2021. I had to live off my past earnings for a month and for the first time in my life I had to go on a government benefit. I cannot walk constantly for long so I have not got another job yet. I did sit and feel sorry for myself, did not walk much, I did not have work to go to so walking has become a bit more difficult and painful. I have had an occupational therapist and a physiotherapist tell me that I need to go for two half hour walks a day.

I have looked online at jobs but most of them look pretty physical. I also did go and apply for a bus driver job, it sounded good and the boss at the bus place seemed pretty impressed by my work history, full drivers licence for sixteen years, because I have had my vaccinations for the Covid virus and that I work well with other people. I just got asked to get my heavy traffic licence and my passenger endorsement. I was so upset when I was at my neurologist, I told her I feel poor and unhappy that I am not at work and I told her the organisations I had applied for work to. I was then told that I will not get a passenger endorsement because of my MS neurological health condition. The tears were flowing and I was very upset being told that, I did end up crying when I talked to my neurologist and the nurse. My neurologist told me that she was sorry and patted me on the arm.

I went away and thought of other jobs that I could do. I also went to Workbridge, an organisation that helps people get jobs who are unemployed. I have a disability because I cannot walk far for very long. I have asked if I could get a sit down job part time. I have just created my Curriculum Vitae for work and we will continue to look for work for me.

CHAPTER EIGHT

New Man and a Miscarriage

I NEVER BOTHERED using protection when I was dating a guy, I saw no point as when I was in past short relationships I never got pregnant either, I really thought that I could not get pregnant anyway. So I am dating a guy, we do not live together we always catch up a few times a week. We always talk about anything and everything, laugh and we get along so well. We even would watch television at 7pm to watch a New Zealand favourite show Shortland Street.

I remember one day towards the end of September 2021, I had cramps down in my stomach and in my nether regions. Also a missed period but I put that down to stress. My boyfriend said to me that I might be pregnant, I doubted it. I did soon after go and get a test and it was positive! I was super happy and so was baby's dad. I thought that anytime I mentioned "my baby" it felt like I was talking about somebody else's baby, that is just the way it was and what I was used to. I went to the doctor and saw the nurses who gave me pregnancy leaflets and numbers of midwives to contact, then the doctor who advised me to contact neurology at the hospital and they went over my medications.

I got told that all my medications were ok apart from Gabapentin, the nerve medication I used to have before bed every night.

I carried on and took my Elevit medication each day because they had folic acid and iodine in them. I had my thirty sixth birthday in Wellington because my brother shouted me and my mum up there to visit him. We went to Te Papa, the Wellington Zoo and we toasted marshmallows on the beach at night. It was so nice and my brother, sister in law and wee niece made me feel so welcome and happy.

I did end up going to the emergency department for light bleeding and spending seven hours there. They did tests and ordered a pregnancy scan for baby. Me and my boyfriend went to the scan and we could see a little sac with baby in it, this was my first time ever to be scanned for a baby.

The next time I went to hospital I was there for twelve hours where I was observed and had more serious bleeding. I was informed for the first time that baby had no heartbeat. I was in hospital until the late morning where I saw the Early Birth Unit. There was a way that would naturally dispel baby and there was a possibility that I could have to come back afterwards to the after-hours emergency department for baby not fully coming out or an infection. They did tell me about doing the procedure where baby is cleaned out of me under anaesthetic. I was also told I could keep baby's remains if I wanted to so I could bury them. I chose not to keep the remains and underwent my operation the next day. It was not allowed to drive because of the anaesthetic, so I got a taxi to and from hospital with my mum. My boyfriend was an hour out of town working so he could not come, so my mum came with me.

We named baby the gender-neutral name Ashley because at six-seven weeks it was too early to tell baby's gender. We were going to get this beautiful half-moon crib that was out of town, it was so gorgeous and I wanted to get it for baby. I have thought that we could get a small tattoo with a half moon, Ashley and the date of my operation – so we can remember baby forever, Ashley will never be forgotten. My boyfriend agrees and we are planning to make a trip out of town to go and get the tattoo from my tattooist friend.

I have joined online miscarriage groups to speak to other ladies so we can support each other through our baby loss. Yes baby loss is quite a regular thing but I do hope to never experience it again, it was horrible. The feelings that I get when I think of baby Ashley, I miss what never got to happen and there have been many tears shed over this. I do hope I can have babies in the next few years – I love children! Watching them grow, teaching them things, reading to them and having a little laugh with them. I am known as "Aunty Bex"to my family and friend's children.

CHAPTER NINE
Disability and 2022

I WAS WALKING fine in 2020 and had a relapse, had medication and things did improve. Then my walking started going downhill with the stresses I had upon me with the separation marital act, work wanting to dismiss me for my health reasons and how long that process took. I could walk fine sometimes and other times I needed my walking stick. I was very unhappy about this and rarely went out anywhere. I did realise though that my walking started to be more difficult and painful. So I had occupational therapists and a physiotherapists working with me.

That stopped and I sat around, doing voluntary work and yearned for my old life. I really did want a job as my student loan was big.

I can still drive my automatic car and I have a disability parking permit. I love to go driving but due to the price of petrol I may need to slow down with the need for going for a drive.

My dad had a serious stroke in July 2022. We were not in close contact with my dad but we all went to Christchurch Hospital to see him and bid him farewell.

My nephew was born in August 2022. I was so happy for my brother and sister-in-law and was happy to meet him in October 2022. He's so cheeky and I love his blue eyes, they're so beautiful! My mum and I bought him a Mometoes hand and feet casting, I love it!

My divorce proceedings were this year too. I signed a one party divorce and I had to get a private investigator to serve the divorce papers on my ex-husband. This was done and I asked the private investigator how the delivery went. She said she knocked on the door and his mum answered, welcomed her in and made her a cup of tea. She presented him with the papers, he said he knew these were coming, he signed them and she called me to get her $140 and then she would send them to Ministry of Justice. I thanked her and paid her. It was made final in July 2022 and I felt relieved.

Well the days rolled on slowly and I'm grateful that here in New Zealand when it is needed, we can get a benefit to live on. I really did want to get back to work again – to pay my student loan off and to pay for renovations for my house. I signed up for Workbridge and I am in contact with some Ministry of Social Development work brokers. I apply for jobs, get decline emails and I get a few job interviews and I still did not get work.

I finally got my job as a dispatch operator in December 2022 – this was after one and a half years. I do love my new work because it is positive, welcoming and I notice there no widespread ill feeling there, so refreshing! I also use my walking stick, so I am pleased I was given a job. I am so thankful, I just want to be kind to others, meet my responsibilities and to continue giving to others through volunteering when I can.

It has been a crazy ride the last few years – the uncertainty was scary! The mind can think a thousand things, you just want to run and hide and you do not know what is next. So awful, I will never forget it. I did want the ground to open up and swallow me whole more times than I care to count. My divorce proceedings were this year too.

I sold my house in October 2023 because the house had a steep driveway and my mobility is not the best.

It is June 2024 now. It has been three years with Brent and we've still the best partnership through the ups and downs. No matter what though, we support each other :)

Rehabilitation centre is helping me with physiotherapy, they gave me crutches and they said there is spasticity in both my calf muscles. My goal is to strengthen my legs up and walk independently again.

I bought a wheelchair off Trade Me and I use it if I'm going somewhere that requires a bit of walking/so if I am out with family or friends I do not slow everyone down. :)

I did lose my job due to restructuring in March 2024.

I am the "eternal optimist" and I am still doing volunteering work. There is always something out there to look forward to!

Contacts
(If anyone has depression/is suicidal
or knows anyone needing help)

In all emergencies call 111

Lifeline 0800 LIFELINE – 0800 543 354

Life Matters Suicide Prevention Trust – On Facebook

Lifeline 0800 543 354 (0800 LIFELINE) or free text 4357 (HELP) –
Samaritans 0800 726 666

Depression Helpline 0800 111 757 or free text 4202 or
www.depression.org.nz

Healthline 0800 611 116 – for advice

If anyone would like to email/post to me

Rebecca Tupu:
rebeccazhome@yahoo.com

*This is a service that only New Zealand citizens
can access to request assistance.*